Purple ☆ Little

The World's Best BOYFRIEND

GINGER WOODPECKER! ☺

by Purple Ronnie

First published 2009 by Boxtree
an imprint of Pan Macmillan Ltd
Pan Macmillan, 20 New Wharf Road, London N1 9RR
Basingstoke and Oxford
Associated companies throughout the world
www.panmacmillan.com

ISBN 978-0-7522-2697-2

Copyright © Purple Enterprises Ltd, a Coolabi company 2009

9 8 7 6 5 4 3 2

A CIP catalogue record for this book is
available from the British Library.

Printed and bound in Hong Kong

'Purple Ronnie' created by Giles Andreae. The right of Giles Andreae and Janet Cronin
to be identified respectively as the author and illustrator of this work has been asserted by them
in accordance with the Copyright, Designs and Patents Act 1988.

Visit **www.panmacmillan.com** to read more about all our books
and to buy them. You will also find features, author interviews and
news of any author events, and you can sign up for e-newsletters
so that you're always first to hear about our new releases.

...ahhh

a poem to say

I Love You

I thought I'd write a poem

Cos I wanted just to say

That I think you're
really scrumptious

And I love you more
each day

a poem for
A Boyfriend

There's something I think
I should tell you
I hope you don't get a
big head
You're not only gorgeously
handsome and cool
But you're totally brilliant
in bed

Saying I Love You

Boys usually only say
I Love You
When they want to
Do It with you

a poem to say
↓
You're Special

You're a very special person

And you mean a lot to me

When you're around you
make the world

A better place to be

a poem for a

Boyfriend

You're a hunky handsome
heart-throb
You're a fab and groovy
dude
You're a juicy lump of
gorgeousness
A scrumptious plate of food

You're a hot and horny lover

And if I had my way

I would smother you
in chocolate
And feast on you all day

Getting in the Mood

Music is a great way
of getting people in
the mood for Doing It...

a poem about ↓

Missing You

There are times when I
really do miss you
And think of you missing
me too
So I close my eyes tight
And I daydream
That I am together with
you

lovely
daydream

a not too soppy poem to say
↓
I Love You

This poem says I love you
And you make my life
                 complete
Except for all your
                 bottom burps
And your stinky feet
♡

Important:-

When boys come round to your place, why does all the food suddenly disappear?

a poem to say

You're Wonderful

I know that it sounds
cheesy
But I'm telling you it's
true
It's fab to have a lover
Who's as wonderful as
♡ you

a poem about

Love

When you love a person

You love all their
different parts

But I just can't love
the odour

Of your after-curry
farts

<u>Important</u> :-

Try not to dribble too much when you are snogging...

...dribbling is not sexy

a poem for a

Gorgeous Man

I wanted just to tell you

That you're my perfect
man

You're so handsome, cool

☆ and gorgeous

And I'm your biggest fan

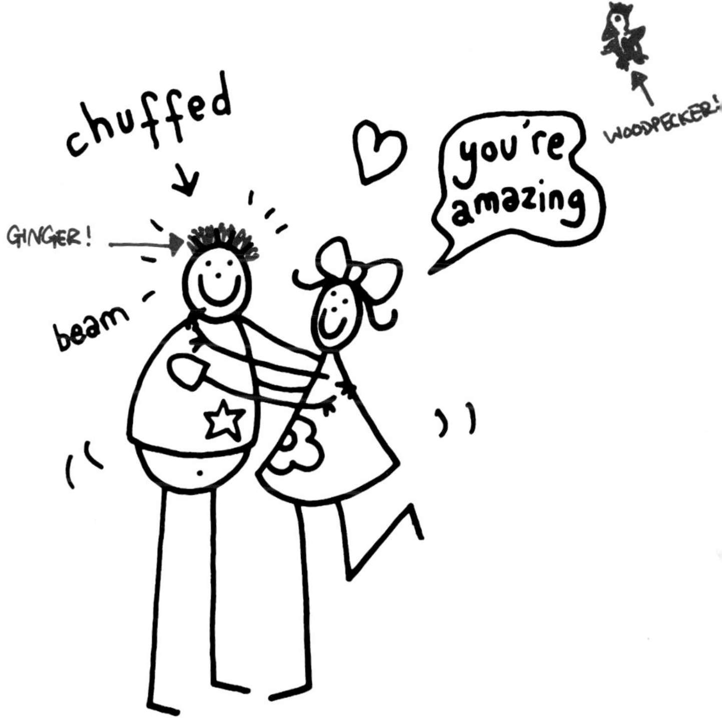
chuffed
GINGER!
beam
you're amazing
WOODPECKER!

a poem about

Trousers

Men just don't know how
to turn women on
Though they try to excite
and arouse us
They should be romantic
and caring and kind
But instead they just
tear off their trousers

Annoying Things Boyfriends Do

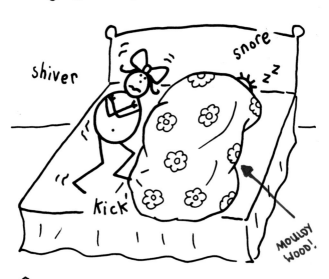

1. Hog the blankets

2. Forget your birthday

a poem to say
↓
I Love You

Sometimes when it's late
at night

And we're alone together

I want to take you in
my arms

And cuddle you for ever

♡

SWEATY PANTS!

a poem about being

Smelly

You take off your shirt

And your armpits are
whiffy

You take off your socks

And your feet are all
niffy

You give me a hug
And you're terribly
smelly
Then you ask me to kiss
you
- NOT ON YOUR NELLIE!

Sport

Boyfriends waste at least half of their lives watching sport

a poem about

Love

Sometimes it makes you
feel happy
And sometimes it makes
you feel blue
But I find it makes me feel
smashingly fab
And that's cos I'm in it with you

a poem about

Letting Off

Some people get lots of
pleasure
From books or from music
or art
But you seem to think it's
fantastic
To just have a really
good fart

Other Girls

Never trust a boyfriend who says he doesn't fancy other girls...

...he's fibbing

a poem for

My Lover ↓

The smashing thing about you

That makes me think
you're great

Is you're not only my
lover

You're also my best mate

a poem about

First Dates

When it comes to Doing It
Most girls like to wait
But boys want full on
                nookie

By the end of their first
                date!

When Doing It with someone for the first time it is always best to use protection

LEEDS UNITED!
'ere we go
'ere we go
'ere we go
Beer
ale
Beer
Beer
Beer
ale
ale

a poem about a

Football Fan

Why do men talk about
football

When most of them don't
even play?

They chant and they cheer

And swig loads of beer

And just watch it on telly
all day

a poem about

Listening

I love how when you look at
me
Your eyes begin to glisten
But I sometimes wish that
when I talked
You'd use your EARS and
LISTEN!

Yak Yak
Yak and then...
yeah...whatever
flap
flap
Blimey!
SPORT
ETC
OUCH

The Bathroom

Boys make unbelieveable smells when they go to the lav

They always leave the
seat up

And they <u>never</u> clean
the bath

a poem about

↓

The Bathroom

Floss flecks on the mirror

Pube hairs on the loo

Girls can see these clearly

Why can't boys see them
too?

a poem about

Cuddling

Girls don't try to wind
boys up
Or get them in a muddle
But sometimes all they
want
Is just a cosy kiss and
cuddle

Surprises

Some people make
Doing It more exciting
by taking their lover
by surprise

big squeeze

BABY! ☺

Watch out f